NETWORD 3

TEACHING LANGUAGES TO ADULTS

Mixed ability teaching:
meeting learners' needs

Susan Ainslie

Cartoons by Joanne Bond

The views expressed in this publication are the author's and do not necessarily represent those of CILT.

Acknowledgements

The foreign language co-ordinators and adult education tutors and students in Lancashire who participated in the Lancashire survey; David Selby and the other members of the steering group who supervised me while I was an advisory teacher; and Ute Hitchin of CILT, who made many invaluable suggestions while this book was in preparation.

First published 1994
© 1994 Centre for Information on Language Teaching and Research
ISBN 1 874016 33 X

Cover by Logos Design and Advertising
Printed in Great Britain by Bourne Press Ltd

Published by the Centre for Information on Language Teaching and Research, 20 Bedfordbury, Covent Garden, London WC2N 4LB.

Contents

Introduction

Adult education language classes almost invariably include students of a very wide range of ability, motivations and needs, more than any other sector of education; many classes succeed or fail according to the tutor's skill in responding appropriately to this challenge. Learners should be at the heart of any educational process, and it is vital that tutors should be able to differentiate between individuals within their groups and help each learner to achieve his or her learning potential.

The initial impetus to write this book arose out of ideas put forward by tutors as part of a survey into foreign languages in adult education in Lancashire[1]. The book starts by discussing what 'mixed ability' means, and goes on to propose a range of strategies to help the tutor to manage it successfully. It also suggests ways in which students can be involved in making decisions about the learning strategies they should adopt, as part of the underlying aim of encouraging them to become independent learners.

It is hoped that this book will be useful for teachers who are working in relative isolation, but also for groups involved in training and in-service courses. There are a number of suggestions for practical activities which may be undertaken by the individual teacher or may form the basis for group work.

---

1. See Ainslie S, *Foreign language courses for adults - the Lancashire survey* (1991) - unpublished report available from the author at Edge Hill College, Ormskirk, Lancashire.

What do we mean by mixed ability?

Chapter 1

What we understand by the term 'mixed ability' is not confined to differences in the capacity to learn between different individuals. It includes variations between individuals in a number of separate areas, some related specifically to potential for language learning, but many much broader and yet perhaps even more significant for what happens in the classroom. It is one of the particular challenges of adult education to cater for the needs of every individual in a group.

The key areas included in the term 'mixed ability' may be summarised as follows:

- **Motivation, interests and needs**
  Why did the students join the class in the first place? Have those reasons changed as the course has progressed?

- **Linguistic ability**
  Some students are better language learners than others, and previous language learning experience will have varied considerably.

- **General educational background**
  Was it a positive or negative experience? How long did it last? Did the students acquire any study skills?

- **Learning style**
  Students learn in different ways.

- **Age**
  Is one ever too old to learn?

- **External pressures and time available to study**
  How can we cope with a group which includes some students who do nothing outside lesson time and some who spend two to three hours a day studying?

- **Anxiety**
  Lack of confidence and nervousness can hinder progress.

Teaching adults can be one of the most rewarding forms of teaching. In almost all cases learners come to classes highly motivated, and motivation is widely recognised as the most important factor in language learning success. Unfortunately, the motivations, interests and needs of one student are unlikely to be the same as those of another, and in any group, particularly of adults, the range is likely to be extremely wide.

Motivation, interests and needs

Motivation may be **instrumental**, which means that there is a specific, practical reason for learning. This may be because the learner is trying to sell spare parts for cars in the country of the target language, has a grandchild who cannot speak English, or wants a qualification in the language because it will enhance job prospects. Motivation may also be **integrative**, which means that the learner is interested in and willing to share some of the attitudes and attributes of members of the other linguistic community. The language is being learned for its own sake, rather than for where it can lead. Students may also be attending a class for reasons which have nothing to do with learning a language and yet are just as important, for example to get out of the home for a few hours or to keep the mind alert. Furthermore, learners' motivations often change as the course progresses; a satisfactory way of filling in Tuesday evening may turn into a keen interest in learning the language as soon as a sense of achievement begins to develop.

The specific **linguistic needs** of the learners may also be very varied:

Needs are not only linguistic: students also have **psychological and social needs**, which will vary from one individual to another. If students have joined the class because they want to make new friends, opportunities must be created for them to get to know their fellow students. A group that is socially successful is likely to achieve more linguistically than might originally have been expected. Learners need to feel emotionally at ease in the language learning environment; the teacher must ensure that they do not, for example, feel

The need for foreign languages is extremely diversified, depending on the country, class, age and occupation of the learner, as well as on the language required, the situations and conditions of use and the kind of knowledge and balance of skills that the learner will need to be able to bring into action[2].

2. See Trim JLM, 'Languages for adult learners', in Kinsella V (ed), *Language teaching and linguistics: surveys*, pp 101-120 (CUP, 1978).

fear at the prospect of speaking in front of the class. This aspect of 'mixed ability' is considered in more detail below under *Anxiety*[3].

Linguistic ability

There is often a very wide range of linguistic ability in an adult education class. Students in a beginners' class in a popular foreign language, French for example, usually range from those who have never studied a language before to the learner who admits after the course has been running for several months to having done five years at school. In addition, some will have quite a good grasp of grammar, but have great difficulty putting sentences together; others will have picked up a number of phrases and words on holiday or from friends, but have no idea of the structure of the language.

Someone who has already studied a foreign language - whatever that language might be - will be more linguistically aware than someone who comes to a class with no experience of foreign language learning. A beginner in an Italian class who has previously learnt French for several years is likely to be able to deduce patterns in Italian far more readily than the learner coming to the Italian class who has never studied a language before.

In addition to the differences in starting level, progress will also vary enormously, as some people learn languages more easily than others. This may apply overall, with some learners finding all aspects of language learning more difficult than others, or it may apply to particular skills. Some find it easier than others to produce the sounds; some remember more easily than others; some find it extremely difficult to write with any degree of accuracy; some have considerable problems understanding the spoken word. Some learners have great difficulty applying language patterns (grammar) and accepting that ideas are expressed in different ways in different languages. They look for equivalences between languages, word for word translations.

Linguistic awareness will vary according to the background of the students. On the whole, however, learners who have never studied their own language, nor attempted to learn another, are unlikely to have any appreciation of how language is constructed, nor be aware of any rules being applied. As teachers we need to be particularly careful with learners

3. See Sidwell D, 'Recognising the learner's needs', in Arthur L and S Hurd (eds), *The adult language learner*, pp 12-19 (CILT, 1992).

in this category. The concepts of 'verb', 'subject' and 'object' are difficult; 'direct' and 'indirect' objects are a nightmare even to many advanced students! This is one reason why it is so much more effective to define our objectives in terms of competences rather than in grammatical terms. In other words, it is preferable to say what our learners will be able to **do** (get something to eat and drink; express opinions; ask questions; etc) rather than what they might **know** (the present tense; interrogative constructions; etc). It is not always necessary to use grammatical terms to teach learners how to communicate, particularly at lower levels.

Previous educational experiences will have left all learners with a whole range of expectations and possibly fears. They may have had an enjoyable and successful experience of education, a negative experience of failure, or something in between.

General educational background

Within adult education classes we can expect to find learners who left school at fifteen with no qualifications and no subsequent experience of formal education in the same group as those who stayed in full-time education until their early twenties and may have attended a number of courses since.

Extended time in formal education **ought** to mean at the very least that the learner has developed effective study skills but, as this is not always so, we do need to spend time discussing strategies for effective learning. Adults who have been a long time out of education may also have forgotten how to make the best use of time available. What may seem to us to be self-evident, that it is better to spend a little time studying every day rather than to do everything in one long session, may not be obvious at all to our students.

Whatever their previous experience of education learners will come to classes with a number of preconceptions about what 'education' is or ought to be. Some will expect a formal teacher-centred approach and may be ill at ease working in small groups rather than always being tutor led. Some learners are hostile to a communicative approach (*I don't want to play games; I came here to be taught.*). Referring to activities as 'communicative exercises' rather than 'games' makes them more acceptable. It also helps if course members are given clear explanations as to why they are being asked to undertake a particular type of exercise.

Learning style

People learn in different ways. Some want a formal approach and may well want to understand every word. There is usually someone in a class who specifically asks for grammar. Others are quite happy to let the new language wash over them and seem to learn without having everything explained. Some learners seem unable to learn unless they can write it down. Some need the support of a group before they can begin to learn, while others learn quite happily on their own. Some need a lot of reassurance and can be discouraged if something is presented to them that they find difficult, while others welcome the challenge.[4]

Age

There is a popular misconception that adults beyond a certain age are too old to learn, and that their memories begin to fail. There is one sphere of language learning in which the adult is at a disadvantage over the child, and that is in the area of pronunciation. Many adults who otherwise acquire an excellent command of a foreign language never quite master the new sound system. However, adults generally have a better established and more complex perceptual framework than children, a framework which facilitates both learning and remembering. They have often developed strategies for learning; they may already possess some of the concepts which the learner needs to learn a language successfully.

As we grow older, changes do take place in our capacity to assimilate new information. As we approach the end of our forties, our intelligence begins to crystallise, in much the same way as our bodies lose their suppleness. The effect of this is that the short-term memory (which retains new information for 30 seconds to one minute before transferring it to the long-term memory) becomes more liable to break down through the effects of overloading. It is therefore important to teach older learners a little at a time so that they can transfer new knowledge to the long-term memory in small sections, before moving on to the next piece of information.

While the tutor is presenting new information in very short steps for the benefit of older learners, younger students in the class may become bored and impatient to move on. This is one very good reason why the traditional teacher-centred approach to language learning, with the teacher addressing the whole class for most of the time, is usually inappropriate for adult language learners. Strategies for more differentiated ways of managing classes are suggested in chapter 4.

---

4. See Arthur L, 'Strategies', in Arthur L and S Hurd (eds), *The adult language learner*, pp 46-52 (CILT, 1992).

From a practical point of view, health problems may affect learners of any age, but are more likely in older ones. If any of your learners are hearing impaired, it is important to ensure that they can hear what is going on. Handouts need to be clear enough for everyone to be able to read them.

Within the same group we may have learners who have no time available between lessons to study because of job and family commitments and those who, as work and family commitments have decreased, can and do spend hours each day studying. External circumstances may also affect what happens in the classroom. Those with many pressures or problems outside the classroom may find it difficult to leave them behind when they attend lessons.

Psychological factors can affect progress in language learning at least as much as level of cognitive skills. Self-image, self-confidence and self-belief can make a great difference to language learning success.

Many learners are extremely anxious when they start their course. Anxiety is not restricted to those with little experience of success in other spheres, but may conversely arise in those used to being in positions of authority and control who are suddenly the pupils, knowing much less than their teacher and afraid of making fools of themselves. I have seen an executive director of a multi-national company breaking out in a sweat on being asked in French what his name is.

In courses for industry it is usually not a good idea to put people at different levels in the hierarchy of a company in the same group, as those at a lower level in the hierarchy may turn out to be better linguists. If the office junior makes more rapid progress than the managing director, or a middle manager is more able than a senior executive, it can be embarrassing for everyone and may result in some course members dropping out.

Some class members answer questions whether they know the answer or not, whereas others are petrified at the thought that they might be asked to speak out in front of the class. Dominant class members may indeed have a demoralising effect on the others, confirming their feelings of inadequacy.

The need to differentiate

The definition of 'mixed ability' as discussed in this chapter may be represented by the following diagram.

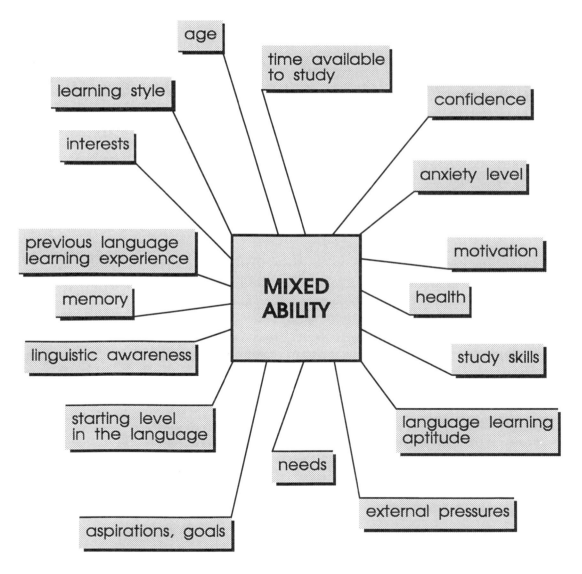

As teachers, we have to deal with all these issues. We need to be able to explain the basics to those who need them, and consolidate them, at the same time as we are challenging and stretching the most able. We have to find ways of enabling each student to learn according to his/her preferred style. We must reassure and encourage those who lack confidence and also keep demanding, overbearing students happy without letting them dominate the class. We need to enable grandparents to communicate with their non-English-speaking grandchildren at the same time as we prepare holidaymakers to get the most out of their holidays and business people to establish a good rapport with their clients. We need to cope with course members who study all day between lessons as well as with those in the same group who do nothing at all. We should remember that we are trying to help learners to become autonomous and encourage them to take part in decisions about strategies to be employed. And we must not neglect the learners whose main motive for joining the class was to make friends.

We are aiming therefore to **differentiate** between our different learners. Differentiation is the process by which teachers provide opportunities for all students to meet their individual needs and achieve their potential.[5] Meeting individual learners' needs does not imply that they never work together: for many adults the support of the group is an important ingredient of the course.

Our first step is to find out as much as we can about our learners as soon as possible; we then need to implement a range of strategies which will respond to the needs of each individual. These will include:

- whole-group work;
- pair and small-group work;
- individual work;
- a variety of texts;
- a range of activities.

If we are at least aware of the variations in our classes as outlined above, then we are probably part-way along the road to dealing with them. The next chapter suggests ways of helping tutors to get to know their students.

---

5. See Convery A and D Coyle, *Differentiation - taking the initiative*, Pathfinder no 18 (CILT, 1993).

Over to you

Task 1   Is there anything missing in the diagram representing 'mixed ability' on page 8? You may feel that in your situation there are other factors which should also be taken into consideration, or some which do not apply. Draw up your own diagram.

Task 2   Consider one of your classes. Can you say something about each member of the group in relation to the various features discussed in this unit?

Name _____

Class _____

A. **Linguistic ability**
  ● starting level in the language _____
  ● previous language learning experience _____
  ● aptitude_____
  ● linguistic awareness_____

B. **General educational background**
  ● learning style _____
  ● study skills _____
  ● previous educational experience _____

C. **Motivation, interests and needs**
  ● linguistic _____
  ● social _____
  ● psychological _____

D. **Age**
  ● memory _____
  ● health _____

E. **Personality**
  ● anxiety level _____
  ● confidence _____

F. **External factors**
  ● time available to study _____
  ● external pressures _____

Stage one: get to know your students

Chapter 2

We cannot implement effective strategies for dealing with mixed ability until we have some knowledge of our students in terms of the definition of mixed ability given in chapter 1. Clearly we will be some way into a course before we know all our learners well enough to be able to say something about every learner for each of the criteria, but we should aim to find out as much as we can as soon as possible, and this process should start before the course begins.

The following strategies will contribute towards a better understanding of our students:

- pre-course counselling;
- questionnaires;
- ice-breaking activities;
- helping students to get to know themselves;
- record keeping.

Pre-course counselling

If at all possible, try to be present to meet prospective class members before or at enrolment. Time available will be limited, but even so an informal discussion can reveal a lot of information which will help you to plan according to the needs of individual learners. The discussion will be a **two-way process**: you give them information about the course so that they can decide whether or not it is what they want. They give you information about themselves so that you can adapt your plans for the course to ensure it meets their needs.

The clearer you can be about the course, the easier it will be for learners to decide whether or not it is the course for them. It is helpful to give students a handout to take away with them, as they will be unlikely to remember everything you say. This should include a brief outline of the course aims, content and learning outcomes, and specific details about any examination that may be taken and information about books that should be bought. For example:

Newtown College
French - Year one

Course tutor:
Class time:
Course length:
Room:

Marianne Smith.
Mondays, 7.15 - 9.15 pm.
30 weeks.
S2 - first floor, main building. Turn right at the top of the stairs.

Date of first class: Monday, **25 September**.

Course details

This course is a beginners' course, and you do not need to know any French at all to join. It is also a suitable course for you if you have done a little French before but feel you need to revise again from the beginning.

The course aims to teach the French you need to enable you to deal with everyday situations on a visit to a French speaking country. You will learn how to introduce yourself and talk about yourself, as well as how to get things to eat and drink, go shopping, ask for and understand directions, travel around, and so on. The course concentrates on speaking and understanding: grammar will be kept to a minimum. A variety of materials and methods will be used and you will be given lots of opportunities to practise in a friendly environment.

The course will be based on the new BBC French course, *The French experience*, and you will need a copy of the book and of the set of cassettes to go with it if you are to make the best use of the course. These are in stock at Newtown Bookshop and cost £xx.xx. Any other materials will be provided by the college. You will also be able to use the facilities at the college's resource centre.

At the end of the course you will be able to take a National Vocational Qualification at Level One.

If you have any questions, please ask me on the enrolment desk.

I look forward to meeting you.

Marianne Smith

When eliciting information about the learner, it is not enough to ask: *What level are you?* A lot of students would reply *beginner* even if they studied the language for several years at school. A better question is to ask for how many years the student has studied the language. You need to ascertain approximate level in the language and any specific reasons for attending the course. It is also important to keep a record of information obtained for future reference by jotting down replies. Extra comments like 'very anxious' could also be noted.

One way of getting information at or before enrolment is to ask prospective course members to fill in a questionnaire. They can do this while waiting in the queue to enroll. As well as providing you with useful information, this has the added attraction of giving them the feeling that they are not wasting too much time queuing. If it is not practicable to do this, however, it can be done at the first lesson.

Questionnaires

A few helpful hints about questionnaires:

- Keep them short and simple - simple to complete and simple to analyse. Ticking boxes or circling appropriate words or phrases makes for easy analysis. Beware of making the questionnaire look like a test as in 'Write a few sentences about yourself in Spanish'. Potential course members may feel threatened by this and be put off joining the class.

- Make sure that all the questions are relevant. Be very clear in your own mind what your reasons are for asking the questions. Do not ask a question if the answer is obtainable from the enrolment form. Many of us are suffering from questionnaire fatigue these days, and there may be some hostility if the point of some of the questions is not obvious, or if some of the information is duplicated elsewhere. (Make sure you have access to enrolment forms. Sometimes they include information that is useful for the tutor, but the tutor never sees them.)

- Make it clear that people are not obliged to fill in the questionnaire or to answer every question.

- Be discreet. Assure learners that any information provided is confidential, and will not be referred to in class - wait for learners to volunteer it. This is not the same as using information to plan appropriate lessons.

Example of a pre-course questionnaire

We would be grateful if you would complete the following questionnaire and hand it in when you enroll. The information you give is entirely confidential. Completing the questionnaire puts you under no obligation to join a class, but it will help your tutor to prepare the course. You are not obliged to answer the questions. Thank you.

Name: _____

1. Which language are you interested in studying? _____

                                                                        YES/NO
2. Have you studied this language before?

3. If so, please tick the statement(s) which best describe(s) your previous language learning:
   [ ]   For a few years at school a long time ago
   [ ]   Up to 'O' level/GCSE/school leaving certificate at 16
   [ ]   A few phrases picked up on holiday
   [ ]   Another adult education class (please give details)_____
   [ ]   Other (please give details) _____
                                                                        YES/NO
4. Have you ever studied any other foreign language?
   If so, which one and to what level?

5. Why are you interested in learning a foreign language? Tick any of the following that apply, but put a 1 next to the most important one:
   [ ]   For holidays
   [ ]   For work
   [ ]   Because I have friends/relatives who speak the language
   [ ]   To keep my mind alert
   [ ]   To have a pleasant evening out
   [ ]   To keep up my standard in the language
   [ ]   Because I would like to have/need a qualification
   [ ]   Because I'm interested in the way of life/culture of the country
   [ ]   Other (please specify) _____

6. Is there any other information which you think would be relevant? (For example, are you hearing impaired? Any information will be treated in confidence.)

   _____

Thank you for your co-operation.

- When you have prepared your questionnaire try to set up a pilot to try it out. Ask as many people as possible to look at it - including a class you are currently teaching if possible. This usually throws up weaknesses or ambiguities which you can then alter before doing the 'real thing'.

- There are invariably some late enrollers. Try to get them to complete the questionnaire as well, otherwise you may miss some important information.

- Make sure, having collected the information at enrolment, that you make time to analyse it before the first class.

A number of texts are available which discuss the design of questionnaires in detail[6], but the safest thing to do is to use or adapt one that has been used before. The example on page 14 has been adapted from one that was used as part of a survey in Lancashire and was completed by 473 course members across the county.

While a questionnaire is one way of getting information about course members without taking up too much of their time, it is clearly only a beginning. Ice-breaking activities are activities whose purpose is to help learners to:

Ice-breaking activities

- start to get to know one another;
- start to recall rusty skills in the language;
- relax;
- lose any feeling of anxiety about being in the class.

They are particularly important at the beginning of the course or after a break. For the tutor, ice-breaking activities provide the opportunity to start to assess many of the features of mixed ability discussed in chapter 1 - linguistic level, interests, personality and so on. The following activities are different means to achieve the same end.

---

6. See Oppenheim A N, *Questionnaire design, interviewing and attitude measurement* (Pinter, 1992).

 **1**

In a beginners' class the possibilities linguistically are clearly limited, though by the end of a first class the exchange of basic information such as names, nationalities and where people live is perfectly feasible if presented during the lesson. Learners at this level will probably need a handout with the necessary prompts to help them. At the end of a first lesson, for example, the following could be given out:

¿Cómo se llama?
¿Cuál es su nacionalidad?
¿Es de Birmingham?

Me llamo ....
Soy ....
No, soy de ....

What is your name?
Where do you live?
Are you English?

My name is ....
I live in ....
No, I am ....

Comment vous appelez-vous?
Où habitez-vous?
Etes-vous français?

Je m'appelle ....
J'habite à ....
Non, je suis ....

If there are students in the group who can manage more than this, they should be encouraged to develop their own conversations.

 **2**

The ice-breaking activity that is used most commonly at a variety of levels is:

Teacher: *Talk to your neighbour and find out what you can about him/her - then report back your findings to the rest of the class.*

Structures required for this activity need to be carefully practised beforehand, perhaps by plenary question and answer and/or by the tutor introducing him/herself first. Students may feel more comfortable if given a list of suggested questions so that they have something concrete to start from and thus feel more confident (see page 18). If we do not prepare carefully at each stage we may increase the anxiety that we are hoping to dispel, as students sit there thinking, *Oh, help. I can't do this!* Having practised in pairs, learners can be asked to present their partner to the rest of the group. At this stage it will be necessary to practise the third person singular.

Teachers with many years' experience may feel that this technique has been used so often that they should find something new. If it is a class consisting mainly of students who have been attending classes for a considerable time, this may well be the case, but for learners new to the situation something simple and straightforward is less threatening than a more complex activity, and the above exercise can provide a lot of useful information about the students.

Hand a questionnaire to students as they enter the classroom, ask them to complete it and then compare their answers with someone else and find out to what extent they are in the same position. They could then report back to the rest of the group. If students are advanced enough, the questionnaire can be in the target language. This is a useful activity while you are filling in registers or dealing with latecomers. The questionnaire can be of the type presented above (page 14), but may also ask the students to consider what sort of a learner they are, by asking them to tick statements or adjectives which apply to them from a given list (see page 22 for example). This can be in the target language or in their native language, depending on the level of the class.

3

Give learners a grid to complete about other members of the class. On the whole, learners will be feeling nervous, so it is a good idea to give them the support of questions written out in the target language. They ask their neighbour first and then move round to others in the class.

4

	1	2	3
Wie heissen Sie?			
Wo wohnen Sie?			
Arbeiten Sie? Was sind Sie von Beruf?			
Sind Sie nach Deutschland gefahren? Wann? Wohin?			
Warum lernen Sie Deutsch?			
Was machen Sie in Ihrer Freizeit?			
Seit wann lernen Sie Deutsch?			

	1	2	3
What is your name?			
Where do you live?			
Have you any family?			
Do you work? What do you do?			
Have you been to England?* When? Where?			
What do you do in your free time?			
Why are you learning English?			

*   If the course is taking place in England - *Which parts of the United Kingdom have you visited?* If the course is taking place in the US, Australia, etc, then this question must be modified accordingly.

	1	2	3
Comment vous appelez-vous?			
Où habitez-vous?			
Que faites-vous dans la vie?			
Etes-vous allé(e) en France? Quand? Où?			
Quels sont vos passetemps?			
Depuis quand apprenez-vous le français?			

They can also be encouraged to add their own questions. The information obtained is subsequently collated in a plenary session.

Alternatively, students may be asked to identify the person with whom they have the most/least in common.

There are many other ice-breakers, though some of them require a fairly confident group of students. Examples include:

- The class sits in a circle and the teacher, who is holding a ball, says something about him/herself, then throws the ball to someone else, who says something about him/herself, then throws the ball to someone else, and so on. If the ball comes back to the same person he/she must say something different.

- Students are instructed to draw pictures of an animal that they would like to be, then discuss with their partner why they would like to be that animal. They then repeat the exercise with others in the class.

- Tell students to find three things that they have/do not have in common with the other members of the class.

  You may feel that you need to give students more help to get them started in this exercise. This could be done by producing a list of topics they might like to consider:
  - Married?/single? - Family - children?
  - Home/garden - type/size/location
  - Car - make/colour
  - Pets
  - Job
  - Food/drink/meals
  - Favourite films/TV programmes/music/famous people
  - Hobbies
  - Holidays - destinations/activities
  - Clothes
  - Reasons for learning the language
  - Politics/current affairs

Or, if you feel students need more concrete support, by providing a list of questions they could ask one another. For example:

- How many children have you got?
- What sort of car have you got?
- Have you any pets?
- What time do you usually get up/go to bed?
- What do you do for a living?
- What don't you like to eat/drink?
- Who is your favourite actor/filmstar?
- What do you do in your free time?
- Where do you usually go on holiday?
- Why are you learning English?

These examples may be more successful as an ice-breaker after, say, the Christmas or Easter break, when students already know one another.

Helping students to get to know themselves

One of our aims is to encourage learners to be independent and to take charge of their own learning. If we can begin to work towards this right from the start of the course, we are more likely to succeed in meeting the various needs of all our learners, because they will be involved in decisions about what they should do.

Learners will not automatically be able to do this and will need help. The first step they need to take is to consider what sort of learners they are. One way of encouraging them to think about this is to ask them at the beginning of their course to complete a self-evaluation sheet like the one below (see pp22-23), first designed at a CILT workshop on autonomous language learning. It asks students to think about what sort of people they are, what sort of learners they are, and what they have particularly liked or disliked in their previous language learning experience. For beginners this would naturally be in their native language. The sheet could then be reconsidered at various points throughout the learners' course. Information obtained from this sheet could help the teacher to define and develop aims and objectives as well as help the learner to become more aware of the process of language learning. The teacher and the student should both keep a copy of the sheet.

Record keeping

It is useful to keep records on the course members, for example a file containing copies of the questionnaires and additional information about individuals as you get to know it. In order to deal with the mixed ability in a class, you can assume that not everyone will do the same work all the time (as we shall see in chapter 4). Keeping an individual record therefore will be essential. The sort of information to note down includes 'extra' work an individual has done, or areas where particular help is needed, or individual students' specific interests. Numbered worksheets help to make the task of recording easier.

New Town College

1994-5

Course: Year 3 - French   **Tutor:** S Jackson

Name: Jane Freeman   **Tel:** 123-7896

Address: 17 Acacia Avenue, Fordingham

1. Reasons for learning/interests and needs
French daughter-in-law. To keep mind alert.
Interested in oral skills - has trouble understanding.

2. Previous experience
Years 1 and 2. A couple of years at school. Visits.

3. Dates absent
27/9 (week 3), 3/11 (week 8)

4. Homework/classwork (numbers refer to the completed worksheets)

1	2	4	5	6	7	9	10	11	12
14	15	16	17	18					

5. Extra work done
1a   2b   5a   7a

6. Areas for development
Use of perfect/imperfect tense: needs more listening practice, particularly when spoken at 'normal' speed.

As part of the task of encouraging learners to become more autonomous, you may consider it to be more appropriate to let students keep and maintain their individual records themselves. You are likely in any case to be encouraging learners to choose at least some of the activities they undertake.

Connaissance de soi

Veuillez remplir HONNETEMENT le questionnaire ci-dessous. Une fois rempli, gardez-le dans votre carnet personnel.

a. Quel genre de personne êtes-vous?
(Cochez comme il convient)

( ) confiant/e
( ) peu sûr/e de soi
( ) persistant/e
( ) paresseux/se
( ) ouvert/e d'esprit
( ) travaillant dur
( ) à l'esprit inquisiteur
( ) nonchalant/e
( ) relaxe
( ) auto-discipliné
( ) timide
( ) arrogant/e
( ) nerveux/se
( ) trop conscient/e de soi
( ) dominateur/trice
( ) modeste
( ) enthousiaste
( ) bien organisé/e

b. Quel genre d'apprenant êtes-vous?
(Cochez comme il convient)

(i) Aimez-vous...
( ) travailler seul/e
( ) travailler à deux
( ) travailler en groupe

(ii) Quand vous ignorez quelque chose, que préférez-vous faire?...
( ) trouver la réponse tout/e seul/e
( ) demander la réponse à quelqu'un d'autre
( ) demander la réponse à votre prof

c. Qu'avez-vous aimé(A)/détesté(D) en tant qu'apprenant/e d'une autre langue étrangère?

(i) Parler dans la langue étrangère
A D à mes camarades
A D à l'Assistant/e
A D devant toute la classe
A D à l'extérieur de la salle de classe
A D une fois dans le pays étranger

(ii) Ecouter
A D le prof
A D l'Assistant/e
A D mes camarades
A D une cassette audio
A D et voir une vidéo

(iii) Lire
A D seul/e
A D à haute voix
A D pour obtenir des renseignements
A D pour le plaisir
A D comme devoir

(iv) Ecrire
A D comme devoir
A D pour le plaisir
A D pour moi-même

Self-evaluation sheet

Please fill in the questionnaire below HONESTLY. When you have completed it, keep it in your personal file.

a. What sort of a person are you?
   (Tick as appropriate)

   ( )   confident
   ( )   unconfident
   ( )   determined
   ( )   lazy
   ( )   open-minded
   ( )   hard-working
   ( )   inquisitive
   ( )   easy-going
   ( )   self-disciplined
   ( )   shy
   ( )   arrogant
   ( )   nervous
   ( )   self-conscious
   ( )   domineering
   ( )   modest
   ( )   enthusiastic
   ( )   well-organised
   ( )   chaotic

b. What sort of a learner are you?
   (Tick as appropriate)

(i)   Do you like...
   ( )   working alone
   ( )   working with one other person
   ( )   working in a group

(ii)   When you don't know something, what do you usually do?...
   ( )   find out the answer on your own
   ( )   ask someone else the answer
   ( )   ask your teacher for the answer

c. What sort of activities have you particularly liked (L) or disliked (D) about learning a foreign language?

(i)   Speaking in the foreign language
   L D   to other members of the class
   L D   to the teacher/assistant
   L D   in front of the whole class
   L D   outside the class
   L D   in the country where the language is spoken

(ii)   Listening to
   L D   the teacher/assistant
   L D   other members of the class
   L D   an audio cassette
   L D   and watching a video

(iii)   Reading
   L D   alone
   L D   aloud
   L D   to find out information
   L D   for pleasure
   L D   for homework

(iv)   Writing
   L D   short homework exercises
   L D   longer homework passages
   L D   letters/cards to friends, to make bookings, etc.

In addition to the formal strategies suggested above, a lot can be learned about students informally, over tea, on the bus, or from casual remarks made in class.

With all the information now acquired, decisions can be made about how to differentiate between the different members of our class. Chapter 3 considers how to get started.

Over to you

Task 1	● Look at the suggested pre-course questionnaire (page 14). Could you use it for your classes? How could it be improved?
Task 2	● What other strategies, in addition to those outlined above, would you use to find out about your learners?

Stage two: getting started

Chapter 3

This book has so far focused very much on the learner rather than on what is to be taught. If we are to be learner-centred in our teaching, the learners and their needs should always be our first consideration, our starting point. One of our main purposes is to set tasks which are appropriate for each individual within the class and this chapter considers how to achieve that goal. It may involve setting tasks that are sufficiently open-ended for the learners to develop them in a variety of ways as they wish; it may involve giving different tasks to different learners. Whatever the strategies we employ, we must be able to differentiate between the different members of our groups. First, however, we need to prepare both ourselves and our course members so that they are in a position to fulfil their potential.

We can do this by:

- **creating the right atmosphere** - relaxed, non-threatening, positive;
- **developing the learners' study skills** - how to make the best use of the time available;
- **involving the students** in what we are doing - discussing what we aim to do, why and how;
- **planning and organising** - core and branching activities, records for each individual;
- **starting small** - try simple activities first and build up confidence.

Creating the right atmosphere

The crucial role of the teacher from the beginning is to convince students that they are going to enjoy the classes, that they are going to succeed and that their dignity will not suffer. The adult classes which work best are those with a teacher who takes trouble to create a relaxed, social atmosphere, who is approachable and who, above all, shows sensitivity in the way that he or she deals with students' errors.[7]

---

7. Howson B, *A vous la France! - notes for teachers*, p 6 (BBC, 1984)

Many tutors made the same point in the Lancashire survey, e.g.:

... build up an atmosphere of mutual respect and self-confidence ...

... create a friendly non-competitive atmosphere ...

... give lots of praise and encouragement ...

An environment needs to be created in which learners do not feel threatened and anxious but are happy to acknowledge that they have different strengths and weaknesses from the other participants and to support one another in whatever way they can. Not only should the tutor make efforts to get to know the learners, but learners should also be given the opportunity to get to know one another as early as possible in the course.

The content of the lessons is crucial if we are to foster a relaxed atmosphere. We should ensure that the level of the work is not too difficult but at the same time stretches the learners, that what we do is relevant for all learners, and that there are plenty of opportunities for them to approach us individually for help and for us to check with them that all is well.

Developing study skills

Some learners will be used to studying, but for many of them formal education has been over for some years and it is therefore important to discuss with them how to learn. Things which may seem to us to be self-evident are not necessarily obvious to everyone. It is also useful to suggest ways in which students may make best use of the time available to them to study between lessons, as some have many commitments in their everyday lives.[8]

As a starting point, it is worth raising with students the importance of the following:

- study between lessons to maintain the momentum and to consolidate what has been learnt;
- spend a small amount of time each day studying rather than a long block all at once;

8. See Doyle T, *Lingo!* (BBC, 1992) for an examination of the way to learn languages.

- keep going over what you have learnt to refresh your memory;
- use 'dead' time, when ironing, washing up, driving, etc, to listen to tapes;
- remember that different people learn in different ways; work out what helps you most, and concentrate on that;
- remember that learning a foreign language is a gradual process, and do not expect too much of yourself too soon.

Involving learners

Whether the methods are new to you or not, they may well be new to your learners. Make sure they understand what you are planning to do and why. Many will previously only have had experience of traditional teacher-centred teaching and may feel that this is the only way that anyone can learn. Objectives and methods need to be discussed not only in general terms at the beginning of the course, but also in specific terms before embarking on an exercise.

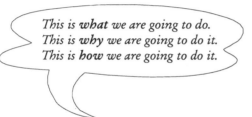

*This is **what** we are going to do.*
*This is **why** we are going to do it.*
*This is **how** we are going to do it.*

At the end of the lesson learners should be reminded of what they set out to do and that they have achieved it. If they are achieving the objectives set by new methods, this recap at the end of the lesson will help to convert the sceptics. Do not assume that course members will necessarily welcome activities you have planned. They may need persuading that what you propose will help them learn. In a new situation many feel insecure, and the effect may be that students become hostile as a defence mechanism and the strategies fail. On the other hand, if you discuss the lesson with them they may be willing to become involved in the organisation of it.

Planning and organising

Planning and preparation are always important. If we are to cater for students' individual needs, we must anticipate that different students will need at times to undertake different activities. This work will need to be organised particularly carefully in advance. The importance of keeping records on each individual student has already been mentioned earlier (see page 20); it is also important to prepare detailed lesson plans like the one below for purposes of class organisation.

As will be seen in the next chapter, many lessons will be divided up into **core** work, which everyone does, and **branching** activities, which student and teacher decide upon on an individual basis. The core work will specify the main objectives of the lesson; the branching activities reflect the personal learning goals of the student. The options available can be recorded on a simple form:

Objective	Learn to talk in the past	
CORE WORK		
CONTENT	**ACTIVITY**	**MATERIALS**
Passé composé with avoir	1. Oral presentation	Flashcards
	2. Plenary practice	OHP of key structures
	3. Pair work practice	Handout of key structures
BRANCHING ACTIVITIES		
Consolidation	Repeat pair work with different partners	Handout of key structures
Advanced	Pair work extending range of verbs	Handout of stimulus questions
Listening practice	Listen to extract from radio programme – answer questions	Cassette player, cassette, worksheet
Reading practice	Reading comprehension	Newspaper article, worksheet
Video	View extract and produce résumé	VCR, video cassette, taskcard
Writing practice	Write card saying what did on holiday	Model postcard to reply to
Business context	Role-play	Handout – specific vocabulary, taskcard

Based on A Convery and D Coyle, *Differentiation - taking the initiative* - Pathfinder 18 (CILT, 1993)

Where possible, the classroom must be set out for the different activities before the start of the lesson. If the classroom you have to teach in has rows of desks in lines facing the front, the desks could be pushed together into groups to make more appropriate working areas for branching activities. The position of powerpoints must be taken into consideration, and it may be necessary to locate an extension lead. Students are usually quite happy to take responsibility for re-arranging the room and for putting everything back at the end of the lesson: if several people are involved it can be done in a few minutes and is well worth the effort.

There are considerable implications in terms of preparation time for teaching in this way. It is therefore a good idea for colleagues to get together, to share tasks and to pool worksheets, resources and ideas.

Do not be too ambitious if you have not tried differentiated work before. Try a straightforward pair work exercise first, involving perhaps just two alternative tasks. Both you and your class need to adjust to the new approach and become confident. If you try something very complex it may go wrong because you are not used to the way in which the class needs to be organised.

Starting small

Group work includes simple role-plays like conversations in cafés or booking hotel rooms, but it can also entail major simulations such as producing a newspaper in the newsroom or reconstructing crimes. More complex activities should not be attempted until everyone is comfortable with straightforward tasks.

Having prepared ourselves and our learners, we are now in a position to develop strategies and devise specific activities to meet learners' needs.

Over to you

Task 1   ●   Look at the list of study skills above (page 26). What could you add to it? How would you recommend that students develop individual skill areas such as pronunciation, listening or reading comprehension?

Task 2   ●   Produce a lesson plan to fit in with the core/branching model above (page 28) for a different learning objective. As far as possible, produce specific exercises to meet your objectives. What additional information do you need to prepare?

Strategies

Chapter 4

It has been established that the focus in the classroom should be on individual learners, by involving them as much as possible in decisions about what they should be doing, and by trying to encourage them to identify for themselves the learning styles and strategies that suit them best. They have, however, enrolled for a specific course and will have some common objectives. On the whole students want to share with others a feeling of progression towards a common goal. That is why the model of core and branching activities suggested in the previous chapter is a useful one, as it enables the provision of communality and individual variation at the same time. This is not to suggest, however, that every lesson should be organised in exactly the same way. There is a range of features within courses which will help to ensure that the needs of all learners are being addressed.

As students learn in different ways and have different needs, it is important to build variety into what is taught. We should vary each of the following:

Variety

- the **media** we use - video, audio, written material, satellite TV;
- **classroom organisation** - plenary, pair and small group work, work undertaken individually;
- **materials** - coursebooks, handouts, pictures, travel brochures, newspaper articles, etc;
- **activities** - information gap, games, role-play, gap filling, Cloze tests (for an example, see p38), etc;
- **levels** - easy work to build up the confidence of the less able, tasks to challenge the most able.

Finally and most importantly, though we can suggest to students learning strategies that they might employ, we cannot be prescriptive. It is, for example, inappropriate to forbid students to write things down as they hear them if that is what they want to do, especially older learners whose short-term memories are less efficient than they used to be. In the words of one learner:

> *My memory is no good anymore.*
> *I felt absolutely petrified when I was not*
> *allowed to write things down.*

We need to explain and present things in a variety of ways to correspond to the different learning styles of individual learners. This may involve presenting things in several different ways in one lesson. In the Lancashire survey one teacher described how she presented new material first in the target language, then went over it again in English for those who might not have understood, then gave a grammatical explanation for those who wanted one. She made sure that all students were aware that as long as they were subsequently able to carry out the tasks set, it did not matter if some did not understand the grammatical explanations.

An example at a very basic level is:

Learning objective

Changing *du*, *de la*, *des* etc to *de/d'* after expressions of quantity.

Stage 1

Presentation in the target language.

1. Oral presentation by teacher, preferably with visual aids.
   Model sentences in French:
   > *J'ai du vin. Combien?*
   > *J'ai deux bouteilles **de** vin.*
   > *J'ai de la farine. Combien?*
   > *J'ai un kilo **de** farine.*
   > *J'ai des oeufs. Combien?*
   > *J'ai un paquet **d'**oeufs.*

   Examples written on the board or on a handout.
2. Question/answer, using visual aids. To elicit:
   > *Avez-vous du vin? Oui, j'ai du vin.*
   > *Combien? J'ai deux bouteilles de vin.*

Stage 2

Explanation in mother tongue. E.g.
> *What we have just been practising is changing* du, de la, des *etc to* de/d' *when we specify exactly how much we have.*

Stage 3

Grammatical explanation:
> *We call these* expressions of quantity. *If you want to look these up in your grammar book,* du, de la, des *etc are called* partitive articles, *but it doesn't matter if you don't remember the grammatical term.*

When a course is taught entirely through the medium of the target language, explanations can still be given. The teacher must take great care to keep these explanations as clear and simple as possible.

Those learners with an earlier experience of failure in education have probably joined a course with some trepidation. It is extremely important that such a feeling should not be repeated; early success is vital. Setting learners **manageable tasks** and **short-term goals** so that they can see that they are making progress is important if you are not to lose them. Lesson by lesson and even task by task learners must be aware of their learning objectives, must be set a task that is within their capabilities (not everyone in the class will be doing the same task), and what they have achieved afterwards must be clear to them. Early success will boost confidence and can be built on as the course proceeds.

We need to introduce new material in short segments so that older course members and slower or less advanced learners have the time to assimilate it before moving on to something else. The danger is that, by taking care not to overtax less adept learners, we will bore the more able ones. It is therefore advisable to operate a small group system for some of the time. This part of the lesson can be used to consolidate work with slower learners while also stretching the more able by giving them a more complex task to complete. We could even spend some time with this group introducing something new, for example one of the branching activities mentioned already. If it is a standard part of the lesson and students are involved in decisions as to what they need to do, the danger of demoralising the students who always find themselves in the remedial group will be avoided.

If we have a multi-activity classroom with tasks at different levels, with varied content and different media all going on at the same time, our learners are clearly going to progress at different rates and in different ways. This is not necessarily to say that there will be learners who will be much better than others in **every** skill area. Some may have a very broad vocabulary, for example, but have difficulty understanding the spoken word. Others may be able to communicate orally with ease, but be unable to write a sentence without making a lot of mistakes. In schools pupils sometimes spend whole lessons working through worksheets or booklets individually at their own pace. In adult education this is not desirable, as one reason for attending adult education classes is the

Progression: setting appropriate, achievable goals

camaraderie that can develop within a group. We need therefore to keep in mind the principle of core and branching activities, so that at one level the group is progressing together, while at another students are developing their own interests.

This system of core and branching activities is also invaluable in helping with the problem of learners spending varying amounts of time outside the class on personal study. Thus we can say to the class: *Exercises A and B are essential; exercises C and D are desirable and will help you consolidate but will not prevent you from keeping up with the rest of the class.*

Example of a lesson

Our aims and objectives might therefore look as follows:

Aim

- to enable learners to get something to eat and drink in a café.

Objectives

- to understand key vocabulary likely to be on a menu in a café;
- to understand what a waiter/waitress is likely to say;
- to be able to ask for and get something to eat and drink - and pay for it.

It should be possible to achieve these objectives with all learners. The lesson might therefore proceed as follows:

Core work

1. Presentation of vocabulary with flashcards/viewing video sequence.
2. Learners ask for various items - whole-group activity first, using more able/confident learners as models.
3. Pair work practice.
4. Use menus, develop role-plays with whole group.
5. Practise the role-plays in small groups.

Up to this point, we have been involved in **core** work. From now on we move into **branching** work, which may involve any or all of the following:

Branching work

1. Further practice of the role-plays prepared together in small groups. Learners join different groups for variety.
2. One group is given a different menu with additional items. Teacher presents new items as introduction to activity.
3. Small group works at a listening station (several headphones plugged into a cassette player) or around a cassette player if not available, listening to a conversation in a café and completing a worksheet.
4. Group is given a more complex task - with either the teacher or a more able learner acting as waiter/waitress to prompt more complex responses or with a task card requiring more complex language.
5. Reading comprehension tasks are available for any group which finishes early.

Inevitably, by the end of the course, there will be considerable variation between learners in terms of how much they have learned, but they should all have achieved the same objectives at a basic level. Some will be able to deal with the same topic areas at a higher level, or will have developed particular areas of interest.

We can expect the way in which we organise our classes to fit into one of four categories:

Same tasks or different ones?

1. Everyone is set the **same task** but different learners of their own volition will perform it at different levels or in different ways. This is easily accomplished in written work if, for example, learners are asked to write a letter.

In oral work it requires fairly open-ended activities which learners can develop as they wish. Usually the teacher sets up a situation in which there is a problem, everyone in the group has a role, and the object of the exercise is to solve the problem. Examples include:

- one person in a pair would like to go out with the other one, who would rather not(!);
- mother, father and two teenage children have won, say, £10,000 and have to agree how to spend it - each one has different priorities;
- the council wants to put a by-pass round the town through green-belt land, but local residents and conservationists are opposed. Everyone is given a different role at a council meeting, and the group must reach a decision;

- the scene is a cocktail party or a luxury liner; someone is smuggling heroin; Customs and Excise are on board, and the smuggler has to be found.

To prepare for role-plays or simulations, key expressions must be practised in advance. The best way to set up the situation is usually for the teacher to prepare a series of cards on which the outline of the situation as well as the individual role are set out. The difficulty with this sort of activity is that the degree of participation of individual students may depend on their oral confidence, and some might participate minimally. Sometimes one role in a role-play is more demanding or central than another, e.g. the chairman of the council, so it is important to ensure that one of the more able learners performs it. Here are some further examples:

Role-play 1-
The holiday

1 **Situation** - You have agreed to go on a three week holiday with three other people. You meet to decide what to do.
You like the outdoor life, camping, hiking, climbing mountains etc.

2 **Situation** - You have agreed to go on a three week holiday with three other people. You meet to decide what to do.
Your idea of the perfect holiday is lying on a beach, sunbathing and swimming all day, and going out drinking and dancing at night.

3 **Situation** - You have agreed to go on a three week holiday with three other people. You meet to decide what to do.
You are a 'culture vulture'. You like visiting monuments, museums, art galleries etc when you go on holiday.

4 **Situation** - You have agreed to go on a three week holiday with three other people. You meet to decide what to do.
You are very easy-going, do not mind what you do on holiday and want to fit in with everybody else. Unfortunately, you have a health problem - a weak heart - so must not do too much. You do not want the others to know about it.

A **Situation** - A telephone conversation between a customer and a supplier.
You are an importer of exclusive cognacs. You ring a customer - a major hotel chain - to find out why a bill which has been outstanding for several months has not been paid. Threaten to stop supplying cognac to this customer unless the matter is dealt with urgently.

B **Situation** - A telephone conversation between a customer and a supplier.
You are in charge of purchasing for a major hotel chain. You have to deal with your supplier of specialist cognacs. Due to an administrative error the bill has not been paid. Try to pacify your supplier.

This role-play could be more structured, giving participants specific questions, but if so, the language must be carefully prepared in advance, and opportunities for students to perform at different levels will be reduced. If no 'real' telephones are available, students could sit back-to-back for this exercise.

In group work in which all groups are engaged on the same activity, there is a danger that some will finish more quickly than others. The slower workers may get frustrated if they are never allowed to finish a task, while quicker ones may get bored if they have to wait for others to catch up. To prevent this from happening, it is therefore advisable, at least on occasions, to turn to one of the three other alternatives below.

2. Everyone works with the **same material**, but different people are set **tasks of varying degrees of difficulty**.

For example, in a listening comprehension passage, the following tasks - in approximate order of difficulty from easiest to most demanding - could be set for the same passage.

Listen to the recording. Where do you think it takes place, and what could you say about the people speaking?

Look at the list of words below: listen carefully to the recording and put a tick next to a word every time you think you hear it.

Look at the list of statements below: tick the ones that occur in the passage. (*This could be difficult if the distractors - the statements that do not occur in the passage - are close to the right answers.*)

Listen carefully to the passage then answer the questions below: (*In English or in the target language.*)

Below there is a transcript of the recording you are about to hear, with words omitted. Fill in the gaps. (***Either*** *omit particular words you want the students to recognise* ***or*** *do a Cloze test, missing out every 5th/9th/15th etc word according to student ability. You could give them the first couple of letters of the word omitted* ***or*** *list the words underneath the passage out of order and put in some which do not occur at all.*)

Listen to the recording then write a summary of it. (*In English or in the target language.*)

Students may like to choose which of the exercises they attempt; they may also like to try more than one.

3. **Different tasks** can be set based on **different materials**, though within the framework of the general objectives of the lesson. It would on the whole be appropriate to involve students in the decision about which task they choose to undertake.

The differences may be in terms of level of difficulty: for example, a range of different reading comprehension passages may be provided, all relating to the same theme. In dealing with the topic area of holidays, for example, some learners may be given copies of simple advertisements for holiday destinations, some may have more complex brochures, some may be asked to read a newspaper article discussing the pros and cons of a particular area, and others may be asked to read an extract from a literary or historical text set in the particular area or town. Large cities would be particularly suitable for this sort of range, and such work before a trip would also be very valuable preparation. Furthermore, having worked through their different tasks, the students would probably find it interesting to pool the knowledge they have gained.

Tasks may be based on different types of media and/or skill area. Multimedia series such as those produced by the BBC provide video, audio and a variety of text-based materials related to the same learning objectives.

The differences may be based on the different reasons the learners had for joining the course. Thus, for example, in the early stages of a course when we are teaching learners how to make introductions, we start by presenting the relevant expressions for *May I introduce you to...?/Pleased to meet you* etc. Students can then be divided into groups and, armed with the relevant vocabulary, they can practise:

- introducing colleagues to one another;
- introducing family members to another family;
- introducing friends on holiday.

Whatever the situation learners anticipate for the use of the target language, the learning objectives can almost always fit neatly into a range of contexts. If, however, learners are developing languages for business for more specific purposes than to be able to communicate in a range of general and social situations, their needs would usually be met more satisfactorily if they attended a course specifically designed for the business community.

4. Everyone starts with the **same activity**, and once a group has finished, a **supplementary/extension activity** is given to them. Some of the groups may never get to the extension activity.

For example, the task is a reading task, involving using tourist information to plan the cheapest possible journey to a holiday destination. As the first group is finishing, the news is given to them that the ferries are on strike, or that they have just won £5,000, or that there are floods in that area, so that they have to make alternative plans. As a further extension exercise, they may be required to write a letter to the Tourist Board, asking for information about places to stay, and about things they can do while on holiday.

Self-access

Self-access, also called open learning, is an excellent way of dealing with mixed ability and encouraging autonomous learning. It is particularly valuable for adult learners who will generally be highly motivated and therefore likely to take advantage of facilities available for self-directed study. In the Lancashire survey, one teacher regularly devoted about 30 minutes of a two-hour lesson to a workshop in which the learners chose what they would like to do from a range of multimedia materials. Learners contributed in two ways: they made a small financial contribution to the cost of the materials, and they also brought along their own resources to add to the collection.

Ideally, a DIY self-access resource should be built up by all the teachers in one centre working together. Many teachers have quite a stock of their own materials, and it is in the students' interests if staff are prepared to share. Setting up a self-access centre means in the first instance organising the materials that we already have in cupboards, on shelves, in boxes, in such a way as to make them readily accessible to students, when they need and want them. Copies of different teachers' handouts could be pooled; tourist information, old copies of newspapers and magazines can be collected; copies of old examination papers can be made available. Students often make a significant contribution to such resource banks, and some may be enlisted to help catalogue and organise what is available. The only hardware that is necessary is a cassette player to go with copies of cassettes, as learners like to have the opportunity to develop their listening skills.

In order to make everything easily accessible to students, some sort of coding/organising system must be implemented. This may be no more than one labelled cardboard box for French newspapers, one for German ones and so on. Shoe boxes or the lids of boxes containing photocopying paper make good stores for cassettes. A drawer in a filing cabinet with each file labelled, e.g. grammar/by level/by topic, would be easily accessible and makes a good store for large quantities of material, although itinerant teachers might have to use a few box files instead. Having set up self-access facilities, they can be added to and improved as time allows.

Students will need guidance on how to make the best use of self-access materials. This can be given in the form of specific suggestions to accompany particular resources, but should also include general guidance on how to select appropriate materials, and how to tackle, for example, reading passages or listening comprehensions. General guidance should be given not only orally but also by providing suggestions in writing that can be referred to at any time.

Adult education is increasingly moving into larger establishments such as further education colleges or higher education institutions, through which learners may well have access to larger resource areas, which they may attend outside normal class times. If such a resource is available, learners should be taken to see it, shown what is available and given clear explanations as to how it can be used. Adults, with their high level of motivation, often make much better use of such facilities than the 16+ or 18+ students for whom they were probably originally intended. They can be used to develop particular interests, to consolidate work covered in class, to catch up on work missed, to stretch and extend the most able, to provide learning resources in the less-commonly taught languages. These resource areas are usually staffed so that students can be given guidance on the spot.

A typical resource centre will contain a wide variety of the sorts of materials mentioned above, plus a video recorder and videos, perhaps recordings off satellite to watch, a computer for computer assisted language learning (CALL) and, possibly, an interactive video. Such a centre can considerably enhance the quality of courses. In some centres these facilities are provided free of charge for students attending a course; in others, a fee is charged.

Teaching mixed ability does not imply abandoning whole class work altogether. Adults like to feel a part of the class.

> *... they do like a plenary and the development of group cohesion sometimes ...*[9]

Dealing with mixed ability in plenary oral work

And there are ways of dealing with mixed ability which do not involve splitting the group up the whole time. Oral work can be manipulated so that each learner is operating at an appropriate level. However, we must

---

9. Ainslie S, op. cit. (Introduction).

bear in mind that, particularly in the early stages of courses, some learners will be very reluctant to participate at all, for fear of making fools of themselves in front of others. But it may well be that, just as babies learning their first language hear a great deal of language before they start to produce their own, so a considerable degree of learning is going on in some students even though they are not speaking. We should therefore be wary of forcing learners to participate.

On the other hand, some learners, while lacking the confidence to volunteer to speak, will actually want to be asked. Also, if we do not ask for people to answer by name, the dominant class members will end up doing all the talking. It is important for us to try to get to know each of our learners as individuals, to assess which category each one fits into. Usually confidence increases and participation improves when tentative learners make the effort to speak in front of others.

A variety of strategies can be employed in the presentation and practice phases of the lesson.

- Some course members may have already come across the new language, so you could try to elicit it from them rather than just giving it to the group. Use them as models; ask them to take over your role with the class for a time.

- If you are asking learners to deduce linguistic patterns, e.g. using the conditional, make sure that you ask those who are most likely to deduce correctly first - or everyone could end up very confused!

- Ask questions of varying degrees of difficulty and select those most able to answer at each level. Some students may only be able to volunteer a *yes* or a *no* in the language, and this should be accepted, as it probably means that the learner has understood some of what you have been trying to teach if not all.

A word of warning! If you always adopt the tactic of asking the better course members first, the others will quickly work this out, and it may be demoralising for the poor soul you always leave till last, and may also cause bad feeling, so do vary the strategy you adopt. You may find it appropriate to ask simpler questions first on occasions so that weaker students can get the ball rolling.

- Use visual stimuli such as flashcards or overhead transparencies, as these often enable participants to volunteer appropriate language at many different levels. Revealing a bit of a picture at a time and asking learners to guess what it might be can stimulate a lot of language.

- Go round the class asking everyone to say something different about a picture, but in this instance do not leave the weakest students to the end.

Example of an exercise using pictures

Materials

Pictures of famous people cut out of magazines.

Objective

A consolidation or revision exercise of the topic area 'Personal information'.

Method

Go round the class asking everyone to say something about one of the pictures. If necessary, give an example to get things going, ask questions to prompt an answer if ideas dry up or move onto a different picture. Encourage learners to be imaginative and make things up.

The responses that this produces can vary from:

She's a woman. *She lives in New York.*
She's tall. *She is not small.*
She has blue eyes. *She has two sons.*
She is wearing a black dress. *She is pretty.*
She is twenty-five. *She lives in a big house.*
She's an actress. *She likes dancing.*

to:

Yesterday she went to the cinema with her family.
She would like to have married Harrison Ford.
I would like to meet her. Wouldn't you?
Although she is pretty, I like Marilyn Monroe better.
She should have given up acting long ago.

Variations

- Hide the pictures and get learners to guess who the person is, or do the same thing but reveal a bit of the picture at a time.

- If you would like learners to practise the first person, get them to imagine that they are the person in the picture. *I am tall, I have blue eyes*, etc.

- For consolidation or homework, ask the group to write out a description of the person, incorporating as many of the points as possible and maybe adding a few more.

- With a selection of pictures this activity can be used as a basis for group work.

- Get the learners to say everything that everyone else has said before adding their own sentence.

Group work/ pair work

It is difficult to envisage a tutor who is catering for the mixed ability within a class who does not on a fairly regular basis use group or pair work. There are a number of reasons why it is advantageous.

- Students are more likely to ask questions if they are in small groups.
- They are more likely to be prepared to participate.
- Learners can provide mutual support for one another.
- In a small group learners have more opportunity to practise.
- The tutor can move from group to group helping on an individual basis much more unobtrusively than in a whole class situation.
- Moving away from a teacher-dominated situation will encourage learners to be less dependent on the tutor.
- Overbearing personalities can only dominate one small group at a time - a good reason for changing the composition of the groups regularly!
- From time to time a more able learner can act as an extra teacher, helping the less able. This can reinforce the student's own learning.

On the other hand, some learners object to group work on the grounds that all they hear is the imperfect language of other learners. For this reason groups should not be left together for extended periods unless they are being given some external input. In practice, a tutor can usually hear what is happening in most of the groups, wherever he or she happens to be. And if the objective of the exercise is to practise what has been presented earlier, then it is what is being said rather than what is heard that matters. This should be discussed with learners.

Avoid learners feeling they have been labelled. Vary the composition of the groups, otherwise they will quickly pick up that they are the 'remedial' group or conversely the high fliers. In any case, learners' performance will not always be the same; they may be good at some things and less good at others. Variety will help promote a better social mix and provide varied opportunities for mutual support. It can cause embarrassment if learners are always left to put themselves into groups, as someone may never have a partner, and sometimes people are desperate to change partners but do not like to risk causing offence by saying so!

The following are suggestions for forming groups:
- put learners of the same level together and give the different groups different activities;
- put learners together in 'interest' groups and give them appropriate activities according to their interests, e.g. those learning for work; those with relatives - in-laws or grandchildren - who speak no English; those intending to go on holiday;
- put stronger learners with weaker ones; the weaker will learn from the stronger, who in turn will gain in confidence;
- random selection;
- sometimes encourage self-selection, especially at first when learners may be new to the activity and to the class;
- get learners into groups through the use of relevant language. For example:
  A class has been introduced to the simple future:
    A. *What are you going to do tomorrow?*
    B. *I'm going to play tennis.*

After plenary practice everyone is given a piece of paper on which is written an expression, e.g.:
    go to the cinema, watch television, read a book, etc

There are two/three/four identical expressions according to the number required in each group. Learners have to ask everyone in the class:
    What are you going to do tomorrow?
until they find others doing the same activity as theirs. The groups are then formed, ready for group work.

Groups may be named in a number of ways which can help reinforce vocabulary. For example, group according to different colours, names of places in the country, numbers, awkward items of vocabulary in a relevant topic area. For the lesson plan dealt with under *Progression* on page 34, *casse-croûte, kir, panaché, croque-monsieur* would be appropriate. The tutor can usually unobtrusively manipulate the composition of the groups, e.g. by level, by judicious use of this strategy.

Students can be told which group they are in by simply going round the class and saying for example *Vous êtes bleu*, *Vous êtes rouge*, *You are London*, *You are York*, and so on; group names could be written out on cards and set out around the room in preparation. Be prepared for half the students to forget which group they are supposed to be in. If it really matters you may need to keep a record or produce a written list!

There are a number of ways in which the many and varied needs of all learners can be met. They will progress in many different ways; what we must aim to do is to enable them to progress in the ways in which they choose and to achieve their potential. There should be a clear focus on their collective and individual needs which should be reflected in our choice of activity and organisation of groupings. Above all, we should remain responsive and flexible at all times.

Over to you

Task 1	● Look at one of your lesson plans. Are there any ways in which you could modify it to cater for mixed ability?
Task 2	● Look at your schemes of work. What strategies could you employ to ensure that they differentiate between different learners?

Example of a two-hour lesson plan catering for mixed ability

Appendix 1

Language level: Year one

This plan includes:
- mixed levels;
- mixed skills;
- variety of content/activities;
- graded tasks;
- realistic tasks; .
- cultural awareness - enhancing knowledge about France;
- encouragement of learner autonomy.

It can be adapted for any language.

Aim: By the end of the lesson the learners should be able to ask for, receive and understand tourist information about places in France of their choice.

Some weeks before this lesson, ask for volunteers to write to places in France requesting tourist information. (Have some of your own available as well.) This could be related to a trip someone is actually planning.

Lesson plan

Introduction

Phase 1
- Ask learners for the names of **places** they need to know when they visit somewhere for the first time (e.g. *le camping, la gare, l'hôtel, le café, la plage, the campsite, the station, the hotel, the café, the beach*, etc). Write a few key items of vocabulary on the board or OHP as they arise.
- Then ask what sort of **information** they would want about these places (e.g. *un plan de la ville, une liste des hôtels, un dépliant, des distractions, a town plan, a list of hotels, a leaflet, entertainment*). Include key phrases like *il y a/avez-vous?, there is/are, have you got?* Again write key vocabulary on the board.

Phase 2
- Use realia for initial practice of vocabulary. Share out available leaflets, one per student. Ask questions to elicit basic vocabulary, e.g.:

Question:	*Avez-vous une liste des hôtels?*
Answer:	*Oui, j'ai une liste des hôtels.*
Or:	*Non, je n'en ai pas.*

Question:	*Have you got a list of the hotels?*
Answer:	*Yes, I've got a list of the hotels*
Or:	*No, I haven't got one.*

Question:	*Il y a une piscine?*
Answer:	*Oui, il y a une piscine.*
Or:	*Non, il n'y en a pas.*

Question:	*Is there a swimming pool?*
Answer:	*Yes, there's a swimming pool.*
Or:	*No, there isn't one.*

- Ask better learners first, or give a model yourself of basic verb constructions if necessary.
- At the end of these two phases, give out a handout of key expressions.

Listening exercise

Material
- Recording of conversation(s) in tourist information office (e.g. from *A vous la France*, unit one, video and audio, and/or unit five - slightly more advanced - p 101 in book).

From this point on, learners are given the opportunity to select the particular activity they do, or in this instance have an opportunity to find out about a place in France/England that may be of interest to them. Being given some freedom of choice encourages them to be autonomous, but the teacher will in practice at this stage in the course still be guiding, encouraging and suggesting appropriate activities for many students.

Tasks
Learners can select which of the following they do:
- write down all that they can of what is being said, in French or in English;
- write down what is being asked for;
- with a handout of expressions used on the recordings, but out of order, learners have to listen and write down a number next to each one in the order in which they hear them.
- hand out a list of different things only some of which are on the tape, and learners have to tick the ones they hear.

Learners could decide which one(s) to do after hearing the recording once.

Group work

Preparation

To prepare for this exercise, set out before the lesson one table for each of the different places for which information is available. All the information relating to that place is laid out on the table. Course members divide themselves into groups of four, choosing the place they are most interested in. Anyone who found the listening task difficult should if possible be given the opportunity to go over it again, using a cassette player or a listening station which a few can sit round together.

Those who move on to the group work start by doing a reading comprehension exercise so that they can familiarise themselves with the information that is available. The worksheet could be in the native language if the students cannot cope with the target language, but on the whole someone in the group will be able to deal with the following worksheet, and the teacher will in any case be on hand to help.

Task

- You have French/English friends who are trying to decide where to go on holiday. Look at the information you have and answer the questions to give them an idea of what the place is like.

    Nom de la ville
    - *C'est où en France?*
    - *Il y a combien de campings?*
    - *Il y a un restaurant aux campings?*
    - *Il y a un magasin aux campings?*
    - *Il y a combien d'hôtels?*
    - *Quel est le prix maximum d'une chambre?*
    - *C'est où?*
    - *Et le prix minimum?*
    - *Où est-ce qu'on peut nager?*
    - *C'est combien?*
    - *Il y a des distractions pour les enfants?*
    - *Il y a des distractions le soir?*
    - *Qu'est-ce qu'il y a d'intéressant à faire dans la ville?*

Or:

Name of the town
- *Whereabouts in England is it?*
- *How many campsites are there?*
- *Is there a restaurant at the campsites?*
- *Is there a shop at the campsites?*
- *How many hotels are there?*
- *What is the maximum price of a room?*
- *Where is it?*
- *And the minimum price?*
- *Where can you swim?*
- *How much is it?*
- *Is there entertainment for children?*
- *Is there entertainment in the evening?*
- *What is there to do in the town?*

- If time allows, an individual worksheet for each place can be prepared, but this is very time-consuming and a standard worksheet as above is quite adequate. Where the information is not available, the question can be missed out. Dictionaries should be available. Learners should be encouraged to add other information if they want it. In this exercise they are operating at different, albeit fairly elementary, levels, co-operating to find answers to the questions.

- If time permits, groups can then be asked to split up into two pairs and form new groups. The new groups then exchange information about their respective towns.

- Finally, one person from each group can give a brief summary of what the group has managed to find out. This will be where the most able will be chosen. In this plenary session, if there are any learners in a position to have a discussion in French/English, they can be asked to say which of the places they would prefer to visit and why.

Group work (continued)

Follow-up

Follow-up exercises, to be chosen by the learners, can be to write about one of the places, to write off to somewhere else, to take away some of the information that someone has not had time to look at and study it before the next lesson, perhaps repeating the group work task.

If sensitively handled by the teacher, even work at a very elementary level can unobtrusively be varied to suit the different individuals within the class.

The responsibilities of management

Appendix 2

> *Some of the problems of mixed-ability teaching are in fact caused by inept administration.*[10]

Every group contains a mix of abilities to some extent. However, even if they cannot control anything else, managers **are** in a position to define the language level required for entry to the course, and if they do not do so they can expect considerable drop-out. It is not reasonable to call a course 'Italian' and expect the teacher to cope with, say, beginners and 'A' level students in that group. Meeting the needs of all the learners in the group will still not be easy, but an appropriate structure of language classes within the college, centre or company can help to keep the task within manageable proportions.

A teachers' meeting in Lancashire produced the following requirements of management:

Managers ought to ensure the following:

- effective marketing and enrolment;
- clear course titles and descriptions of course aims and content;
- coherent structuring of courses.[11]

One way of ensuring that there is a coherent structuring of courses is to choose appropriate forms of accreditation so that learners can progress

---

10. Rogers J, *Adults learning*, p93 (OUP, 1989).
11. These key requirements were identified in Lancashire as part of the survey *Foreign language courses for adults*, op. cit. (Introduction).

from one clearly defined level to the next. Routes of progression into higher education should also be established.

Learners should know what they are letting themselves in for before they commit themselves: they should be able to see possibilities for progression over a number of years; they should be properly counselled; they should have a range of options available to them so that they can find a suitable class. Where numbers do not justify a class in less common languages or at higher levels, neighbouring colleges should co-operate to offer a complete range between them, rather than all being offered in one establishment.

What you can do   If you feel that the framework provided within your institution is not appropriate, there are ways in which you can try to improve the situation.

First, does your institution meet the three criteria set out above? If not, try making some constructive suggestions to the head of centre, the foreign language co-ordinator or another appropriate person. The manager may not be a linguist, and may be delighted to receive some ideas.

Get hold of leaflets, newspaper advertisements and other material about the courses you teach. Were you involved or consulted about what should go into them? Do they give a clear indication of the course aims, objectives and content? How could they be improved? Is a clear line of progression apparent? Are you involved in enrolment and marketing? Do you meet the learners before their courses start? Are you able to spend time with them discussing their needs and explaining the requirements of the course?

It is likely to be the case that if the criteria set out above are being met, drop-out from classes will be reduced, and the students are more likely to enjoy and learn from their courses.

Accreditation

Appendix 3

Funding for courses is increasingly to be based on the skills students are able to demonstrate, and teaching and learning are to be more closely monitored. Accreditation does not nowadays necessarily mean taking an examination; there are moves towards coursework-based forms of assessment. In these, the learner who has achieved a particular objective carries out a task which demonstrates what has been achieved. Accreditation can be obtained in individual skill areas, or at different levels in different skills. In a mixed ability class this is particularly useful, as students will be assessed when they are ready, not when the examination board dictates. Individuals may be assessed at different times. This form of assessment is less threatening than traditional ones. In practice, many students are hardly aware when they are being assessed; if an appropriate form of accreditation has been chosen, the sort of activities they undertake as assessment exercises are likely to be the same as the ones they have been doing in class anyway.

Quite apart from the funding issue, accreditation of this sort is to be welcomed. We need to have a coherent structure to our courses and learners need to be able to see a path they can follow if they wish to progress, on to higher education if they wish. There is often a place for raising learners' expectations and encouraging tentative aspirations, rather than just being responsive to perceived need.

Coursework-based assessment requires teachers and students to keep detailed records, to be produced as evidence of what the students have achieved. The importance of record keeping was mentioned in chapter 2, and if we embark upon a coursework-assessed course, we must record everything that is done carefully and accurately from the outset.

Further reading

Ainslie S, *Foreign language courses for adults - the Lancashire survey*, (1991) - unpublished report available from the author at Edge Hill College, Ormskirk, Lancashire.

Arthur L and S Hurd (eds), *The adult language learner* (CILT, 1992)

Buckland D and M Short, *Nightshift: ideas and strategies for homework -* Pathfinder 20 (CILT, 1993)

Convery A and D Coyle, *Differentiation - taking the initiative -* Pathfinder 18 (CILT, 1993)

Doyle T, *Lingo -* video and book (BBC, 1992)

Hamilton J and A McLeod, *Drama in the languages classroom -* Pathfinder 19 (CILT, 1993)

Howson B, *A vous la France! - notes for teachers* (BBC, 1984)

Kavanagh B and L Upton, *Creative use of texts -* Pathfinder 21 (CILT, 1994)

Kinsella V (ed), *Language teaching and linguistics: surveys* (CUP, 1978)

Oppenheim A N, *Questionnaire design, interviewing and attitude measurement* (Pinter, 1992)

Page B (ed), *Letting go - taking hold: a guide to independent language learning by teachers for teachers* (CILT, 1992)

Rogers J, *Adults learning* (OUP, 1989)

Thorogood J and L King, *Bridging the gap: GCSE to 'A' level -* Pathfinder 7 (CILT, 1991)

Tierney D and F Humphreys, *Improve your image: the effective use of the OHP -* Pathfinder 15 (CILT, 1992)

My own ideas